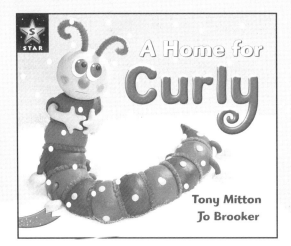

Walkthrough

Read the title with the children, pointing to the words. Then read the authors' names.

Remind (or tell) the children who Curly is.

What might the book be about?

What can you see on the cover?

Walkthrough

This is the back cover – let's read the blurb together.

'Will Curly find a home?'

(Prompt for suggestions.)

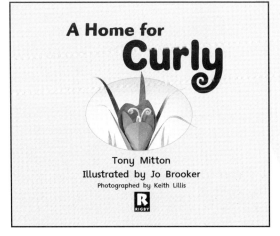

Walkthrough

Read the title with the children, pointing to the words.

What can you see in the picture?

Can you see Curly?

These are the names of the author, the illustrator and the publisher.

Walkthrough

Curly is looking for a home.

He meets his friend the snail.

The snail is telling Curly that his home is a shell.

What is snail saying to Curly? ('*My ...*')
(Make sure the children use the words 'home' and 'shell'.)

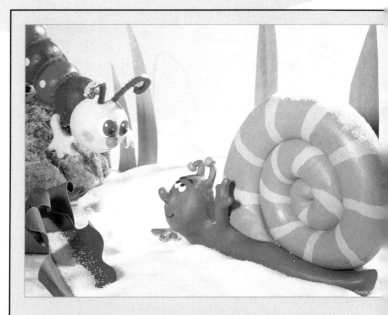

2 My home is a shell.

 Observe and Prompt

Observe one-to-one correspondence.

Does the word 'my' alert the children to the pattern of the text?

If the children say 'house' prompt them to look at the
letter 'm' in 'home'.

Walkthrough

Curly meets his friend the worm and the worm says, 'My …'.

My home is a hole.

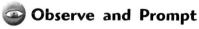 **Observe and Prompt**

Check the children have picked up the pattern of the text.
Check for one-to-one correspondence.

Walkthrough

What does the spider say?
Look at Curly's face. How does he feel?

My home is a web.

Observe and Prompt

One-to-one correspondence is particularly relevant here as children are likely to say 'spider's web'.
Note any self-correction as a result of one-to-one matching.

Walkthrough

The beetle says …

Look at Curly's face now.

How does he feel?

Why is he feeling quite sad?

My home is a stone.

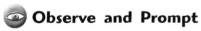 **Observe and Prompt**

Prompt initial sound of the word 'stone'.

Walkthrough

Whose home is a leaf?

What does the ladybird say?

Do you think Curly will find a home?

My home is a leaf.

👁 Observe and Prompt

Observe one-to-one correspondence.

Observe reading of high frequency words, especially 'my' as a lead in to the sentence pattern.

Walkthrough

Curly has found a home.

What is he saying?

Point out the dots.

Model rising intonation and quick page turn.

My home is . . .

Observe and Prompt

Note the use of the pattern as it carries on to the next page.

Are the children able to understand that the sentence carries on?

Walkthrough

Where is his home?

Point out exclamation mark.

How does Curly feel now?

a flower!

Observe and Prompt

Observe one-to-one correspondence.

Observe children read with expression.